WHAT IF I AM?

The 4 Stages In Life... FOR TEENS!

KASHAUN COOPER SR.

What if I Am?
© 2014 by Kashaun Cooper Sr.

ISBN-13: 978-1497383586
ISBN-10: 1497383587

PRINTED IN THE UNITED STATES OF AMERICA

This book is dedicated to
teens and young adults
all over the globe…

Ma Kayla,

You Are So special.

You were created to Succeed!!!!

Remember you will, you must
Accomplish your goals if you
Believe in Yourself!!!!

Khloy Sk 8/14

Acknowledgments

First and foremost, I want to thank my Creator, my God for giving me the strength to push forward and write this book. Abraham Lincoln stated, *"I promised my God I will."* Thank you President Lincoln for that statement. I too have adopted that same life's promise.

Next, I would like to express my deepest gratitude to a woman with a purpose. A woman that has decided to "live life in drive" Ms. Cindy Williams; the founder and CEO of the Baltimore Based non-profit Loving Arms, Inc. Thank you so much for the love and care you share with families from all over. You truly have a heart of pure gold.

Lastly, I would like to thank all the teenagers that I've interviewed for this book. It was you that helped make this dream a reality. I felt your pain as well as your joy. Many tears were shed during the interviews. However, there were also many laughs. I am super proud of you all. Once again, thank you so much for your transparency. You are indeed a lifesaver!

Join The Discussion

I would love to hear your reaction to the stories in the book or something that you may have learned. Please let me know your favorite story and how it affected you.

You can email me at thefourstagesinlife@gmail.com

You can also join in on the conversation and share your success stories or life issues on "The Four Stages in Life" forum available at this address:

www.fourstagesinlife.forumotion.com

"Life is like a camera... Just focus on what's important and good... Capture the good times. Develop from the negative things and if things don't work out... Take another shot"

~ Unknown

Introduction

Such A Masterpiece

Success has always been and still is a topic that I find extremely fascinating. On second thought, maybe it's really not success that fascinates me, as much as it is how people succeed that really leaves me speechless. To hear of an individual or group of teens who have succeeded against all odds; when everything in their environment is screaming give up, throw in the towel, is thoroughly exciting. To see a person ignore the easy road which ends with a white flag raised up saying, "I quit." It can be so inspiring and give you the much needed strength to take action and push forward. To watch an individual trample status quo, demolish mediocrity and emerge as champion, I find that to be extremely amazing. I believe that every teenager has within them their personalized secret to success. Therefore, after reading or hearing about this person's "starting from the bottom" background I think to myself, how and why? These two questions always come to mind after hearing about such great success. Why did they do it? And how did they do it?

Recently, I had the wonderful opportunity to conduct a workshop for teens based off of my first book titled, *"What If I Am? The Four Stages in Life."* It was for a group of fifteen teens. We met once a week for a total two months. Due to the length of time I spent with the teens I had an opportunity to learn in depth more about each teen's life. I learned so much about them including their likes and dislikes. I also learned how they've reached their current point in life.

In the beginning some liked me and there were others that did not want to hear a single word of what I had to say. Luckily for me and them, I had a decent amount of time to help assist them with the process of "living life in drive". After the completion of my "living life in drive" series it caused me to take a good look at my own life in regards to challenges and obstacles. I can confidently say that I have been through a great deal of unfortunate circumstances, both as a teen and an adult. But after listening to the life stories of the teens, I was left with no other choice but to call them warriors.

Even though the group of teens haven't yet reached adulthood, they have learned how to persist like a true warrior. I am convinced that the warrior's mindset isn't age specific, it is action specific. It was the actions of the teens that compelled me to write this book. I used to say that you're never too old to "live life in drive". Consequently after working with that amazing group of teens, it helped me realize that you are also never too young to "live life in drive".

In this book you will read stories of teens who have shared portions of their life that I hope will help you get a better understanding of why the youth in our society are so angry, bitter, broken or hurt. It will also help you understand why amongst our youth there are low high school graduation rates, partakers or victims of violence, drugs and sexual activity that is on a rampage. Let me be clear and state that I am in no form or fashion condoning the actions of the teens in this book and the ones that aren't. I do believe that at a certain age, a young age at that, human beings should take responsibility for their actions. However, I do understand that with every effect, there is a cause. It's called the "why factor".

The same way I ask "why" when a teenager succeeds against all odds is the same way I ask "why" when he/she surrenders to all odds and become enslaved to his/her circumstances. It's been said that circumstances doesn't make the person it simply reveals who the person really is. Truth is, most of us, teens and adults have done some question-able things where it appears that we had become our circumstances. At one point or another we allowed life to define who we were as a person; doing so was totally inaccurate. Truthfully, it is the other way around, it is our job to define life.

Throughout your reading journey in this book you will learn how at one point or another how the teens became their negative circumstances. The good news is, not all of them stayed their circum-stances. Their circumstances did not make them bitter, it made them better. It made them warriors. It made people who are no longer victims but who are now victorious, winners over their circumstances. Yes these teens will go through more challenges and some more difficulties as they grow, but guess what, they can say, "If I made it through that, I can make it through this."

As you read this, you also may be going through a stormy period in your life and it feels as if all hope is gone. You may feel all alone. So I encour-age you to use the teens' testimonies in this book as a model for you to push forward in life. No one ever said that this would be easy but I guarantee that pushing forward is worth it. You were created to succeed. You were created to win. Don't be fooled by your present situation. As bad as it may appear, your struggle wasn't designed to strangle you. It was designed to grow you, to prepare you to help move society further along. You are not very much different than the teens in this book. They do not possess anything more than you. However they do possess the dream and desire to be more, achieve more, do more, and live more.

Keep in mind, when life happens as it will, remember to "ride the storm." Last year while spending some time in Georgia I got caught in one of the worst thunderstorms that I have ever experienced. Mind you, it was a late night thunderstorm, meaning pitch black! I was sitting on the passenger side scared out of my mind. I couldn't see anything in front of me, behind me, or to the sides of me. If I couldn't see, I know good doggone well the driver couldn't see either. I was getting antsy, tapping my feet, and holding my head. I was scared. Nervousness and fear had a strong grasp on my optimistic vision. Bottom line, I felt hopeless, but that was me, not the driver. The driver kept pushing forward. She kept driving against all odds and guess what? We came out on the other side. So when you are feeling scared and don't know what quite to do and the storms of life are becoming overwhelming, hold on to the words spoken by TD Jakes *"there will never be a storm in life that you go through, that you won't come out of on the other side."*

During those weak, lonely, and hopeless moments don't you ever forget that you are stronger than you think! The Creator intended for every teenager to succeed, including you my fellow teen warriors.

It's A Lie: Don't Believe It

One of the greatest things that have ever happened to me outside of building a relationship with the Creator was the day that I stopped believing the lies. Sadly, lies have a way of comforting you for the moment making you feel good only temporarily. In the long term, it destroys your future of a healthy relationship. For years I believed these lies and honestly, there wasn't anyone there to tell me otherwise. So all I had at the moment were lies. At the time of believing these blatant lies, I was unaware that they were lies in the first place. I thought it was the honest truth. Nothing in my environment gave me any reason to believe differently.

Looking back I realized that it was those lies that kept me from becoming my best. As you will read later, it was those lies that kept me from believing in myself and setting goals. It was those lies that kept me living in park, reverse, and neutral. It was those lies that kept me from pursuing my passion and discovering my purpose. I believe it is those same lies that have possibly done the same thing to you.

On the flip side, it's not a good feeling once you find out that you have been lied to. You feel like a fool. There's a feeling of betrayal. You may even ask how could you? Why would you? I thought you cared enough about me to always tell me the truth. The bottom line is that you feel hurt. Let me stop and ask you, what if the person telling these lies wasn't outside of you at all. All along it was the person inside of you. What if it was you telling yourself those lies that kept you from "living life in drive"?

As I stated earlier, I've been there before. For the most part we have all been there before. Each and every one of has an inner voice and all have inner conversations. I bet you are having an inner conversation right now as you are reading this book. Your inner conversations are your thoughts. Your thoughts can be your best friend or your worst enemy. Your thoughts can compel you to believe in yourself or always doubt yourself. Here's the deal, you can control your thoughts. Human beings have the wonderful ability to control our life by controlling our inner conversations. Unfortunately, most don't! We allow life to control our thoughts, our inner conversations which cause us to begin believing certain lies.

When we let life control our thoughts we believe self-lies such as, I'm not good enough. I don't deserve happiness. I am not unique or special. I'm not worthy of love. My dreams and goals are impossible. Lastly, my circumstances dictate my future. The six self-lies mentioned have been known to keep any and every teen who believes in them from "living life in drive". However, here is the irrevocable, immutable, and irrefutable truth. You were created to live your precious life in drive. No other stage will suffice. Yes, you may transition through the other stages but the goal is not make it your home. Your home is "drive". Special things happen while living in drive. You are special so why not live in "drive". You are special so why not live in a special place.

If you need a little help breaking free from the self-lies, this book is here to help you. The teens in this book at one point or another told themselves one or all six of these self- lies. Not only did they tell themselves lies, they believed it. Eventually they got fed up with their situation and they began crushing each lie, one lie at a time. That's exactly what we are going to do before we continue further in the book.

It's time to begin the process of the destroying the self-lies you may have been telling yourself. There is a possibility they you will need to re-read this section multiple times until all the lies stop. If that is the case do so as many times needed to destroy the lies that have been holding you back or will try to hold you back. Re-read it, take notes, write post and stick them up so you can see them every day until your new truth is embedded in your spirit.

Let's Begin the process

LIE #1
I AM NOT WORTHY OF LOVE

Honestly, it took me a very long time to say the words, "I love you Kashaun". I was eager to say "I love you" to everyone else other than the most important person in my life, ME! You may ask, Kashaun why so long? For me it was physical and verbal abuse as a child which led me to believe that I wasn't good enough. For you it may be something different. The truth is, that was my past, it's over and I chose to do something about it. That something was to accept, forgive, and move on. For many years, my past prevented me from seeing my future. However, I knew that if I were to become the best me, I had to let go and begin the journey of loving me.

So remember these words, "Your task is not to seek for love, but merely to seek and find all the barriers within yourself that you have built against love."

You are most definitely worthy of love!

LIE #2
I AM NOT ENOUGH

My question is who says you are not enough? Maybe there were people who told you this repulsive lie like a parent, friend, your partner, or even yourself. Whoever it may have been, it's not true! People's opinion and belief of you does not define you! As long as you are making every effort to become your very best, you are on the right track. The truth is, you won't reach your destination overnight, but you can always change direction. Always remember that you are more than enough. You are good enough. You are smart enough. And you are definitely beautiful and handsome enough! You are a gift and more than enough!

LIE #3
I DON'T DESERVE HAPPINESS

Surely, happiness is our birthright! However happiness is intentional, it is a choice. I love what Julius Marx, American comedian and television star asserted. He declared, *"Each morning when I open my eyes I say to myself, I, not events, have the power to make me happy or unhappy today. I can choose which it shall be. Yesterday is dead, tomorrow hasn't yet arrived. I have just one day, today and I'm going to be happy in it."* I agree with him. There is no shortage of happiness. All we have to do is believe and know that we deserve it. Begin creating your happiness.

LIE #4
I AM NOT UNIQUE OR SPECIAL

This was a constant lie I told myself. I constantly compared myself to my friends, envying their uniqueness. You know, every now and then that inner voice will challenge you, confront you and try to hold you back. That's when you need to let your heart guide you. That's why I decided to have a long heart to heart talk with myself which lead me to discover that I too am unique and special in my own way. So I say to you that you deserve to wear a smile in your heart. Not because of what you have or what you do, but because of who you are. Yes, you are changing each day, but you are always amazing just as you are!

LIE #5
MY DREAMS AND GOALS ARE TOO UNREALISTIC OR IMPOSSIBLE

Nelson Mandela, Civil Rights Activist exclaimed, *"It always seems impossible until done."* British actress and humanitarian Audrey Hepburn asserted, *"Nothing is impossible, the word itself says I'm possible."* The truth is that you and I weren't put on this earth not to break even. You're here to break records and most importantly shatter limits. Think about the women, children, and men who have accomplished what many considered impossible.

Men and women have climbed 29,029 feet above sea level to conquer Mount Everest. Astronauts travel on average 238,857 miles to land on the moon. Long ago men dedicated twenty years of one's life to construct the great Pyramids in Giza. The first flight by the Wright Brothers in 1903 flying only a few seconds, then later in 1905 through perseverance, managed to fly for 39 minutes traveling for 24 miles. There are many more countless "impossible" stories that proved to be possible. You see, positive thinkers see the invisible, feel the intangible and achieve the impossible.

SELF-LIE #6
MY CIRCUMSTANCES
DICTATE MY SUCCESS

The year 2011 was truly challenging for me. Everything that could go wrong did all at the same time. There is a familiar saying "when it rains, it pours." That's all fine and dandy when you are protected from life's downpours. However, that wasn't the case for me. One day while depressed, sitting at the feet of hopelessness, I read an inspiring magazine article about a man who was orphanage at the age of seven. He suffered greatly and found himself in the middle of unfortunate circumstances. Amazingly, this same man was able to pull himself out of poverty to become an author of over 60 books and earned degrees from both Boston and Harvard University. So today believe I am bigger than anything that can happen to me. Remember that your circumstances do not dictate your success.

Now that you have begun the process of destroying your self-lies, it's time to go on our journey into the lives of the teens in this book. You may see yourself in part of the story, or the entire story. The ultimate goal is to see you as winning. Don't forget if you must go back and re-read the self-lies destroyer section, by all means help yourself. Let the journey begin...

The Breakdown

There are four basic stages in life. These four stages are **park**, **reverse**, **neutral**, and **drive**. Truth is, each and every one of us, no matter our background, age, religion, or nationality are in one of these four stages. As you read the book you will discover how each teenager traveled from stage to stage in life until they arrived at the ultimate stage, drive. While reading the brief breakdown below, begin thinking about your life as a teen, the stage you are currently in, and where you desire to be.

PARK

This stage represents hurt, fear, resentment, regret, and hopelessness. The teen living in this stage may have experienced a traumatic event(s) causing them to want to give up emotionally and in some cases give up living life all together. This teen decides that they would rather remain in park than to ever be hurt again.

REVERSE

This stage represents two types of teens. 1) The conformer. 2) The confronter. The conformer is the teen that allows their past to ruin their hopes of a bright future. Instead of the conformer creating a new future, he/she decides to live in the same ole past. Past relationships. Past hurts. Past anger.

They would rather conform to the old instead of embracing and creating the new.

Then you have the confronter. This teen addresses his/her past, not run from it or conform to it. The teen that confronts their past uses their past as a reference point; looking for ways to learn from their mistakes and poor choices. By the teen choosing to learn from his/her past, they can now begin the process of creating a better and brighter present; which will ultimately lead to an extraordinary future.

NEUTRAL

This is the stage where life rules you; the most dangerous stage to live in. Reason for, at times it looks and feels like drive, but in all actuality it is neutral. In this stage, outward influences such as life and peer pressures controls this teen's life rather than inward personal initiative. Surrendering to peer pressure happens often, if not most of the time in this stage. Unfortunately, dreams and ambition also dies in this stage. Possibly, teens living in this stage may also experience a lack of purpose and loss of identity. Unfortunately, this stage can be so dangerously attractive that many teens once they get to this stage, never make it out.

DRIVE

This is every teen ultimate stage to live in. Teens living in this stage could have possibly been tempted by the many different elements of peer pressure. Maybe for a short while they gave in to the peer pressures of life. But something happened in their life which triggered an attitude of refusing to get stuck. Teens "living life in drive" will tell you that living life in drive is not always easy. But it is worthwhile. They may even say challenges, discouragement, and setbacks are going to come. But with a positive can do attitude, determination, and tenacity you will be able to overcome just about anything that come your way. And sooner or later you will achieve your goals and dreams.

THE OVERCOMER

Blair Taylor

KC: **Currently, at this very moment, Blair Taylor what stage in life are you in?**

BT: Now 17 years old with a smile I can say that I am living life "Drive"!

KC: **Please explain why do you feel that you are drive?**

BT: I know that I'm in drive because I am an overcomer. I overcame everything that I've been through so far and it has truly helped make me into the person I am today. I am a better person! I'm about to graduate from high school. I have two jobs. And my goal is to go to college and graduate. So, I feel like my life is going the way I want it to go as of right now.

KC: You know how some people say life is like a roller coaster, journey, or battle, etc. In your opinion, from your perspective how or what would you compare your life to?

BT: I would say life is unpredictable. You don't know what could happen when you wake up. It can be so unexpected. Therefore, I live life day by day, step by step, and minute by minute.

KC: For a brief moment let's get a little personal. If you don't mind, please take us back to a time in life when you were almost knocked down emotionally.

BT: It was when I left home at the age of 15. And stayed away for a year. I stayed with my 19 year old boyfriend which was very abusive. Being with him brought me down. I stopped going to school. I stopped doing what I was supposed to do. When I ended up in the hospital I realized that this wasn't the life that I wanted to live and I was better than that.

KC: You just said a mouthful Blair. You telling me you left the house at 15 years old?

BT: Umm Hmm

KC: **So... were you put out? Did you leave home willfully?**

BT: I left home.

KC: **Why?**

BT: I left because my mom got married. Our relationship wasn't the same after she got married and I felt like she put my stepfather feelings before mines. That really hurt me! So I left.

KC: **Did you like your stepfather then?**

BT: No, I never liked him!

KC: **What about now? Do you like him?**

BT: They're not together. And No I still don't!

KC: **Question, where is your biological dad?**

BT: He passed away when I was 12 years old.

KC: **Leaving the house at 15 years old is a huge deal. All because your mom marries a guy that you can't stand. Did your stepfather abuse your mom? Was he abusive to you?**

BT: He wasn't physically abusive to me. But we was verbally abusive and I didn't like it. I felt like my mom would take up for him and I'm her flesh and blood.

KC: **Can you give us an example of what he said that made you angry or even hurt your feelings?**

BT: It was when he called me a b#tch.

KC: **What did that do to you when he called you a b#tch?**

BT: It hurt my feelings because he said it in front of my mom and she didn't do anything about it. So that just put the icing on the cake. That moment right there had me thinking that she didn't care about me like she used to.

KC: **Talk more about this relationship that you were in at 15 years old. Was it a serious relationship?**

BT: Yes, I was with this person for 3 years. I was young. I was stupid in love.

KC: **You mentioned abuse as it relates to this relationship. What's that about?**

BT: I felt like my mom didn't care about me anymore. I was stuck on trying to find someone that I thought loved me. I was really stuck in that relationship. I say stuck because I could have gotten out of the relationship but I was living life in park. I was looking for someone to love me. But I was looking in all the wrong places. So I find this boy that I thought I fell in love with and actually thought that him and I would be together forever. But quickly, a couple of months into the relationship he just changed.

KC: **How, what was he doing that made you begin to look at him with the side eye?**

BT: He became over protective. Then started being abusive, hitting me and stuff. If I didn't do what he wanted me to do he would just hit me.

In this relationship I ended up in the hospital more than five times. The last time I ended up in the hospital I had to break up with him because I knew that it was best for me. I knew that if I would continue in this relationship he would end up trying to kill me or even worst, killing me.

KC: **What type of injures did you have?**

BT: He would cut me with knives. Bang my head against things. My nose was broken three times and bruised ribs.

KC: **When did the idea of I gotta leave him take place?**

BT: I remember the day and year. It was April 12th, 2011. I was at his mother's house with him and his friend. I didn't do what he wanted me to do. So he told his friend to hit me. So his friend hit me first, then they both started hitting me. I had to go to the hospital because I hit my head on the concrete. I had fractured ribs and needed stitches.

When my mom came to visit me in hospital, I saw the hurt in her eyes. I knew then that I had to call it a quits.

KC: How close did you get to giving up on life?

BT: I was 16 years old and didn't have nowhere to go. I thought to myself there's no reason for me to be here on this earth. Because I didn't have a home to go to and it felt like no one cared.

Because I didn't have nowhere to go, I did stuff to get locked up! I've been locked up 4 times. The last time I did six months for assault.

I can sit here today and honestly say that I would not have ever gotten locked up, but I needed somewhere to go, somewhere to lay my head. My thought was I have to do something to get locked up. At least it was a place to sleep at night.

KC: **So, what triggered your transition from where you were to where you are now?**

BT: I had to get myself together, sit and think. I said to myself I am better than this! I am very smart. I'm the only 12th grade student in my school that has a 4.0 gpa (grade point average). I can do so many things with my life if I put my mind to it.

Instead of looking in the past and blaming others about how I feel. I had to take responsibility for my actions and start doing what I needed to do to be successful in life. I had to make a change.

KC: **What techniques do you use to keep your life moving forward?**

BT: I don't look in the past. I don't think about what I've done in the past, because that only makes me feel disappointed in myself. And I don't want to be disappointed in myself. I always want to feel like I am doing the best I can to make me a better person.

KC: **Please share your major accomplishment.**

BT: I have a 4.0 GPA and I work at City Hall and I desire to become a lawyer.

KC: **Last question, what advice would you give another teen that has been beaten up by life or feel like given up?**

BT: You have to love yourself before you can love someone else. Never let anyone have control over your life because you won't get anywhere in life. You have to make decisions that's good for you!

Reflective Exercise

"Obstacles can't stop you. Problems can't stop you. Most of all other people can't stop you. Only you can stop you."
~Jeffrey Gitomer

1. Think about a time in your life that you had to overcome a situation.

2. What strategies did you use?

   1)_____

   2)_____

   3)_____

3. How likely would you be to use those strategies again?
   ❑ Not Likely
   ❑ Less Likely
   ❑ Likely
   ❑ Most Likely

LIFE BATTLE
Josh Gibbs

KC: **What's going on Josh? Myself and the readers would like to know as of right now what stage in life are you living in?**

JG: Not too long ago I was living my life in neutral, the stage where you just let life control everything. At one point I was even stuck in the reverse stage always living in the past. Recently I had an opportunity to pinpoint my wrong doings and learning from those things. Because of that my life has now been moving forward. So overall, I'm now living life in "drive".

KC: **In our society we do a lot of comparing. Some comparisons will keep us stuck, others will help us move forward. That being said, is there anything that you would compare your life to?**

JG: I would definitely have to compare my life to hydraulics. There are many ups and downs. Even living life in drive there are ups, downs, highs, and lows.

KC: Please, if you can, take us back to a time or event in your life that almost knocked you down emotionally.

JG: Wow! There are so many of those events. But the one that stands out from the rest is when I learned the truth about my father.

My father was in my life from as far as I could remember until the age of 12. My father always made me happy for some reason. He didn't even have to do much. I really admired him. He was like most of my family, stuck in poverty. But I loved him for his work ethics. He would give me little quotes, even though I didn't understand them then, I understand them now. He had so many high standards and we had fun. He did so much good stuff. He enjoyed coming up to the school. Even the discipline made me feel good because I knew that he cared.

Then one day when I was about 11 years old, it had to be one or two in the morning. My mom woke me up out of my sleep, saying, "come on, we leaving, we are getting outta here". So I got my stuff and my two brothers, sister and I, we all left.

After leaving the house, we go to this big building that looks like a school, but really it was a shelter. Of course, since it was the middle of the night it was after shelter curfew hours. Normally, shelters won't let you in after hours. But my mother was close with one of the workers and she's the person that let us in. Now we're in a room full of seventy (70) people and most of the people smelled awful. Here is the other issue we had with coming in after curfew, there wasn't any place for us to sleep but on the floor. So that's where we slept. When I say that this floor was cold, it was so cold. It was like a gym floor. All we had was a thin sheet and a big pillow with these real itchy blankets. My brothers and sister burst out crying. But I'm looking at them completely clueless. They knew what was going on because they were older than me. While they're crying, I look at my mother and asked her who lives here? You see, I'm still lost. I don't have a clue of what's really going on.

During this time I wasn't in school. I missed my entire 6th and 7th grade. They put me in the eighth grade and graduated me. It was at the end of the eight grade at that.

KC: Hold on Josh, are you saying because you and your family were homeless you missed your entire 6th, 7th, and basically, your entire 8th grade academic year?

JG: Yes Sir.

KC: So help us understand. Where were you and your family staying?

JG: Actually it felt like nowhere. We went back and forth from place to place. I remember going to Boston for a year staying with friends and family.

KC: Wow..

JG: No place to call home has really been my life story.

KC: Earlier you mentioned that you were clueless to the situation. At what point did you realized what was really going on?

JG: While in Boston I'm still lost, oblivious to the fact that I haven't seen my dad in an entire year. All of a sudden, out of nowhere it finally hit me after being in Boston for the year. Something is wrong with this situation. So I asked my mom where is daddy? She said, "F that B!"

So after being in Boston for one year we make our way back to our home city. Ironically we ended up staying in the shelter/community center around the corner from my dad's house. One day my mom say's here is your father's address, go see your father. So I go running with excitement in my eyes and as I'm approaching the house I see my dad coming out of the yard. I speak first looking for him to be excited, he wasn't! He spoke back with the "why are you here" look. Mind you, he's usually embracive, always encouraging me and loving. But this time, all he had was a serious blank stare look on his face, like I was wrong for being around there.

He kept it short saying, "aight" stay in school, get good grades alright. I gotta go. I asked him can I go with him? Abruptly, he said no!

His response affected me so bad because of the length of time that I was away from him. I could have chucked it up to he was having a bad day. But he wasn't, something was going on.

I go back to tell me my mother what just happened, she gives me his number and says call him in one hour. An hour passed and I call my daddy. He picks up the phone and says listen, "I'm not your father! Forget that I was ever in your life. All those little memories in your head, get rid of them. I don't want anything to do with you, your mom, nobody. I don't want y'all nowhere around me. I'm not your father so do not call me daddy no more" and hung up!

What he said caught me so off guard. If you were nearby watching me you would have thought that I just got hit by a car. I was lost for words. I was so angry. That single life event messed me up for months.

KC: **I'm sitting here across this table thinking, those words would have crushed me.**

JG: That's exactly what happened. It crushed my spirits!

KC: **How close did you get to giving up?**

JG: It was that moment right there. The situation with my dad really left us in a bad spot. We were so homeless. We were sleeping on the bus stop. It was crazy seeing kids from school looking at me when I would wake up just staring at me in my face. I would eat chips and candy for dinner. I really gave up.

I started selling and using drugs at the age of 14 along with my older brother. But I will say this, all it took was one life threaten event to happen and I stopped selling and using. I had to get out and I did!

KC: **What triggered your transition from where you were to where you are?**

JG: It was when I was 16 years old sitting around looking at my mother drinking real heavy. I started thinking to myself it has to be more to life than this. I knew we didn't have to live the way we were living. One day I woke up and told my mother see you later and I never returned home again.

KC: **Man you have really been through some things that could have kept you living life in park. So what techniques do you use to go forward, to keep living life in "drive"?**

JG: I spend a lot time by myself, thinking, and listening to my music.

KC: **Your music?**

JG: Yes. I'm a new young artist up and coming in the city. I write my own music and perform as well.

KC: **With all that has taken place in your life I know that you must have many major accomplishments. But we would love to**

know if there is one in particular that you would like to tell us about.

JG: I mentioned that I write my own music and perform as well. I'm excited because I am on tour now showcasing my talent and touching lives at the same time. So joining this tour is a huge accomplishment.

KC: **What advice would you give your fellow teen warriors who may be battling their own circumstances in life?**

JG: Patience, life is going to get better if you have patience.

Reflective Exercise

"Everyone wants happiness nobody wants pain. But you can't have a rainbow without a little rain."
~Unknown

Today is your big day. Showtime begun the moment you woke up.

What three tools will you use to conquer your life's battles?
- ❏ Prayer
- ❏ Patience
- ❏ Understanding
- ❏ Kindness
- ❏ Integrity
- ❏ Workout
- ❏ Read
- ❏ Meditate
- ❏ Positive Conversation With A Friend
- ❏ Other _____

Emotional Roller Coaster

Jessica Williams

KC: Jessica Williams, what stage are you currently living in?

JW: Let me start by saying this, I'm not perfect. I've made mistakes and I will continue to make mistakes. However, to answer your question, I am living in "drive"... I've come a long way. I have overcome many obstacles that came my way. I am becoming more and more independent. I have more self-awareness of who I am in general... Lastly, I understand what I want out of life.

KC: People have been known to compare life to a roller coaster, garden, battle, and a journey. In your opinion what would you compare your life to?

𝒥𝒲: Hmmmm. I would say that my life is a mystery. Although I am in control of what could happen. At the same time my life is like a mystery to me. Because I don't even know what could happen next. I just live.

𝒦𝒞: **Can you take us back to a point in time in your life when you were almost knocked down emotionally?**

𝒥𝒲: Sure, it was when my mother started getting sick. My mom has always been in and out of my life. I would see all my friends close with their moms and have a good mother and daughter relationship. Truthfully, I envied it! I always wanted that type of relationship with my mom. My mom is my heart. I wanted everybody to know that she was my mom.

𝒦𝒞: **Trust me I understand. I feel the same way about the relationship between my father and I... It's a father and son relationship that I don't think will never happen. As much as I would love for it to happen. I don't think he feels the same way. Please continue.**

𝒥𝒲: I was 8 years old when I started noticing the change in my mom. Yup! I was in the third grade when I started noticing my mother getting sick. She kept jumping in and out of relationships. She was being careless. She was a whole different person. They say that she is bi-polar manic. It's scary because all my life this is the person that I would want to be around, and she hurts me? At times it felt like it was her fault, other times it didn't. After she would hurt me, I would question, has she ever thought to herself afterwards what am I doing? Does she really feel sorry? Does she remember? My mother never put her hands on me. But I remember the first time she did, I was like who is this person?

KC: **How did she put her hands on you?**

JW: She beat me with a belt. But when she beat me with the belt, she beat me to the point that my entire arm turned purple. I kept asking myself who is this person? She got worse and worse. Interestingly, when I see myself getting angry or frustrated I see her in me.

KC: **So you see your mom in you when you start getting angry?**

JW: Yes I do!

KC: **Is it because you've been hurt?**

JW: Yes, but more so, I am use to seeing my mom act like that. When she was angry and mad and could not get what she wanted, she would yell at me. Talk down to me and really say some hurtful things.

KC: **You mentioned that your mother would say some hurtful things. Could you please share an example?**

JW: It was the day of my 5th grade graduation. I lived in a strictly controlled environment. I wasn't free to express myself until I got older. My mother or grandmother would pick out and buy my clothes. I had no say so about anything. For this special day my grandmother bought me a cute pair of little girl's wedged heels. As soon as my mother seen them, she started going off. She called me a "hoe". Saying things like, I am trying to be grown and fast. I just didn't understand why. I was confused by how someone that close to me could put me down like that.

God tells us to forgive. But it's hard to forgive when the person is constantly doing the same thing over and over again.

KC: **How close did you get to giving up?**

JW: It was when I got kicked out about 10 months ago. The feeling of being neglected by family. The feeling of being giving up on. The feeling of not being good enough for my family. The feeling of not having people to never call you to check on you to make sure that you're still alive. I asked myself, what did I do that was so bad for you to just give up on me like that? I know I am not perfect. I tried my best to satisfy everyone else but myself. It seems as if everybody I tried to satisfy turned their back on me. I asked myself what was I doing wrong? That's the part right there that really hurt me. I felt like there was no need to be here on this earth.

But I think it happen for a reason. I used to be kind of person that was scared to be by myself. I always felt like I needed to be around someone to be happy. I never really had a happy life. I'd never been close with anyone in my family. It was the feeling of wanting to be loved that has come out in wrong ways. I felt like God was trying to get me by myself. I've learned that it is ok to be with myself and love myself.

It took me a long time to learn how to forgive. I was weak then. I am strong now. I don't feel neglected anymore. 10 months ago I felt weak. 10 months later I feel stronger than ever before.

KC: **Wow!**

KC: **What triggered your transformation from where you were to where you are today?**

JW: I realized that I wanted better. I realized that I wanted more out of life. I realized that I can get it, if I want it. It was the people that talk down to me and talked about me that motivated me. I took on the mindset, "I'll show y'all". I will get a job. Guess what, I got the job. I will get my own place. I'm working on that as we speak. I will graduate and I'll do it on my own!

KC: **What are some techniques that you use so that you do not go back and retrace your steps in life?**

JW: God, praying to him, listening to Him as well. I now take criticism. No one is perfect. Listening to what people are saying about me and if more than one person is saying the same thing then it's time to consider making some changes. I know set goals and keep the things I want out of life in the forefront of my mind.

KC: **Ms. Jessica is there a major accomplishment that you would like to share?**

JW: I sure do. I received a scholarship for $1,000 to go to any school of my choice because of writing an award winning essay.

KC: **Thank you for your time so far. But before we finish do you have any advice that you would like to give to your fellow teen warriors?**

JW: Love yourself. Pick and choose wisely who you bring into your life. Lastly, watch what you allow into your spirit.

Reflective Exercise

"Never make permanent decisions
on temporary feelings"
~Wiz Khalifa

1. Think of three negative emotions that you may have experienced today.

   1)_____

   2)_____

   3)_____

2. Did you allow your emotions to control you or did you control your emotions?

   _____

3. If you did allow your emotions to control you, name one way how you will handle it differently tomorrow.

   _____

Guilt Free
Kelli Parker

KC: **Kelli I hope that you are doing well. Let's get started. Currently what stage in life are you at this very moment?**

KP: I feel like my life is in park. I really do. My life is just falling apart. It feels as if everything in my life is just getting worst.

KC: **Everything like what?**

KP: Well before moving here, I lived in Virginia. Before Virginia I lived in Tennessee. While living in Tennessee that's when my mom passed away. Before she passed away we got into a big argument. After our argument I stopped talking to her.

Right after she passed away everybody blamed me for her death, telling me how I was stressing her out. Honestly, prior to our argument we got along. We had our ups and

43

downs, but we got along for the most part.

Right after my mom passed away I went to go stay my father. That wasn't a good combination. After while he and I got into it. Every time he got angry he would begin blaming me for the death of my mother. One day we got into a big fight and he kicked me out.

Everybody blamed me so much for my mom's death they didn't even want me living in the state of Tennessee or Virginia anymore. I finally moved here with my aunt. But that didn't last long as I would have liked. She didn't want me staying with her either.

They tried to convince me that I was crazy and was bi-polar. I don't know anymore. I just been through a lot of stuff in my past that made me very angry.

For instance, my mother used to choose her boyfriends over me and that use to make me very, very angry. There was this one boyfriend she had, he was so abusive. We used to get in trouble a lot as little kids and I guess he thought he was our dad. He used to put us on punishment for a long time and beat the crap out of us. He would to use anything he could find to beat us: extension cords, shoes, switches any and everything. He would just beat the crap out of me. He didn't treat his own children the way he treated my brother, sister and I. And, he didn't do it around my mother. My mom didn't even know. I'm not sure how old I was when he stopped, but it went on for a long time.

KC: **Was it that event happened that knocked you down and possibly out emotionally?**

KP: Yes. But more so it was when my mom died. I was just done with everything. I didn't want to be on this earth anymore. I stopped going to school. I quit my job. I started smoking weed and drinking.

Also my children are in Tennessee. When living with my dad, he and I got into it. To get back at me, he called CPS (child protective services) on me telling them that I was being violent in front of my children. CPS listened and took my babies away. I can't have my children back until I take anger management and parenting classes as well as, therapy. My daily goal is to get my children back into my custody. The pain of not having my children with me is indescribable.

KC: **At what age did you find out that you were about to be a new mommy?**

KP: I was 15 and scared. When my mom found

out all she did was cry and cry. The second time I was 16. When my father found out, amazingly he was supportive.

KC: Even though you're living in park. Do you feel as if your life is getting better in anyway.

KP: No, I really don't. My life was good when my mother was alive. And not having my children with me really hurts badly.

KC: What techniques are you using to help move you into drive?

KP: I do my best to stay around positive people.

KC: Even with the lemons life has thrown your way I'm sure there has to be major accomplishments that you've had.

KP: You're right I have. But sometimes it's hard to enjoy my accomplishments when I'm still going through hell. But, in middle school and some of high school I didn't go to school a lot. But in the beginning of this school year, because of my high grades they skip me a grade level.

KC: That's right Ms. Genius!

KC: If you could sit on this side of the table

and look at yourself or another teen that is going through their own set of challenges, what advice would you give them?

KP: I would say, keep trying until that one day comes and life starts to get better. That's the only reason why I haven't given up, because I know that one day it's going to get better.

Reflective Exercise

*"Guilt is a destructive and
ultimately pointless emotion"*
~Lynn Crilly

Go back to a time in your life where an event occurred that you still feel guilty about.
List three (3) reasons why you have not let go of the guilt.

1) _____

2) _____

3) _____

List three (3) reasons why you should let go of the guilt now.

1) _____

2) _____

3) _____

LIFE AFTER DEATH

Tiffany Wilcox

KC: **Hey Tiffany, how are you today?**

TW: I'm doing great, enjoying life.

KC: **That's a wonderful response! Alright let's get started. Tiffany, presently we the readers would like to know what stage in life are you living in?**

TW: I am enjoying life in "drive". I control my life. I don't allow my peers to control my life. Here is a quick example. A friend of mine tried to get me to skip out on track practice yesterday. I couldn't do that. My track meet is the 26th of this month. So if I were to miss a practice I would not be able to run. That's a recent example of how I do not allow my peers to control my life.

KC: **Of all the comparisons to life that people have created down through the years, Tiffany, what would you compare your life to?**

TW: My life would definitely be compared to a roller-coaster. There has been so many downs. Then it goes back up. Then down again. Then it goes in circles and repeats itself. My life is a serious rollercoaster. Like the Superman or Batman.

KC: **There's a famous phase that says, "life happens". In all honesty life happens to the best of us. If you don't mind please take us to a place in your life where "life happened". But not only "life happened" it also knocked you down emotionally.**

TW: It was the day that I found my little brother dead in my bed. He was six months old and I was 4 years old when I found him dead. I really didn't know what was going on at the time. I still have flash backs and nightmares to this very day of how that event went down. I would say that event is one of the main reasons I am the way I am at this very moment.

I have to be honest, I still don't know that entire truth. The internet is saying that my mother left him in the basement by himself. But I don't believe that, reason for, my mother had 2 kids already and she never done anything like that before. The internet also stated, that my baby brother died of starvation, dehydration, and bruise ribs. Like I said, in my opinion my mother wouldn't do anything like that.

However, this is what I remember. My mother and I came back home from a party and she told me get ready to go to bed. After that, I went to go pull back the sheets and there he was laying there. Of course I didn't know that he had died. I thought he was sleep. So I tried to wake him up, then pick him up, nothing worked. I then tried to move him over. My mother turned around asking, why is he here? He was supposed to be with his dad. When my mother went to go pick him up, she instantly freaked out. She freaked out in a way that I've never seen before when she discovered that my little brother was laying lifeless in her arms. As a result of that incident my mom went to jail for man-slaughter and 2nd degree murder. After that event I don't remember anything else but going from foster home to foster home.

Because of what happen, I had a total of 12 foster care parents. It would have been great if I could have lived with my dad, but that couldn't happen; in my book I don't have one. I don't know his name, background, or family. Honestly, any man walking around could be my father. I know the details and it's probably best that I don't! All I know is that one day my mother was raped, got pregnant, and then came me. So I am a rape baby.

That event definitely knocked me down emotionally, but there's more.

The one of many foster care parents I stayed with during the time I was going from foster care to foster care, was with my grandmother's brother's wife. I was 8 years old at the time. Another event happened that once again reshaped my life. I walked into the bathroom and saw blood everywhere. I found my aunt's body dead in the bathtub.

So this is the second person that I've found dead between the ages of 4 and 9. (They never told me how she died) But I told myself, and I was very serious when I said this, that if I find another person dead I am going to kill myself. Of course you know after that incident it was time for them to find me a new foster home.

Many years passed and I finally have an opportunity to see my mom after all of this trauma has taken place. I was so angry. I blamed her for killing my little brother. I blamed her saying things like, you're the reason for me living in foster care. You're the reason I don't know my other brothers. The reason I don't know my father, and the court stuff. I blamed her for everything. I blamed her for my emotional breakdowns; the reason I cry myself to sleep every night. Honestly, I still cry myself to sleep. So many times I ask myself how would things be if my little brother was still alive?

KC: **Tiffany, it's amazing to see you still smiling after all of what you have endured. I'm not so sure that I would be able to wear a smile like you.**

KC: **So how close did you get to giving up?**

TW: It was pretty recent. It was last year when my best friend killed herself. We had the same kind of story, but her mother was a heavy drug user. It was so bad. Her mother was also very abusive towards my best friend.

One day her brother called me crying something terrible. He couldn't even get his words out. I asked if he was home. And he was. He told me to come over. Once I got there he told me to go in her room. I walked in and I found my best friend wrist slit hanging from the ceiling fan. She had hung herself with the bed sheets from the ceiling fan. That was the worst site that I had ever seen. That same night I was rushed to the hospital because I overdosed on prescription pills. I had to get my stomach pumped. I later woke up with tubes down my throat. Like I said, the next person I see dead with my own eyes I was going to kill myself. That was my best friend since 3rd grade. I was so hurt. I found my brother dead, my aunt dead, and now my best friend dead. I was truly hurt. I just couldn't take anymore.

However, with all that I've been through things are finally now getting to a place that I want them.

KC: What or who compelled you to keep fighting forward? Where did your motivation come from?

TW: My fight is not only for me, it's for my little sisters too. I realized one day that my little sisters are always around me. They want to go everywhere I go and stick up under me. I can't keep doing what I was doing, because eventually they are going to pick up what I'm doing. If I do positive things, teaching them right from wrong. They will turn out fine. Everything I do is for my little sisters. Especially since I don't have my little brother anymore.

KC: **What techniques are used to keep you from going backwards in life?**

TW: I'm a simple person. I go to the gym or I run around the track.

KC: **Many would agree that it seems as if you have been a warrior for the most part of your life. So I'm sure that there's a major accomplishment you wouldn't sharing.**

TW: I remember in the 7th grade, I won state championship for track.

KC: **Since you are a simple person. What simple advice would you give to your fellow teen warrior?**

TW: You can't let your past hold you back. Trust that one day it may help you create a better future.

Reflective Exercise

*"Live life to the fullest because
it only happens once."*
~Maddi Jenkins

Choose the statement that applies to you.

1a. Think of a family member or close friend
that have passed away.
OR
1b. Consider life without a family member or
close friend.

2. Name one goal that your family member
or close friend would have wanted to see
you accomplish?

_____

3. Are you currently taking steps to accomplish that goal?

_____

****For help with setting your goals and goal
setting strategies I invite you to email foursta-
gesinlife@gmail.com for further assistance.

FAVOR, FAITH, AND FORTITUDE

James Dunlap

KC: **What's up James thanks for stopping by for a quick conversation.**

JD: No problem Mr. Cooper.

KC: **Okay James, let's jump right into a few questions.**

KC: **James what stage in life are you currently living in?**

JD: At this time I would have to say that I am living life in neutral. However, knowing that I am in neutral, I am trying my best to move forward. I have some priorities that I need to get in order. I believe that this is one of the main reasons why I am living in this stage.

KC: James, how do you feel about always giving life your best?

JD: We should always be living and striving for the best, even when you receive the worst. When receiving the worst our job is to weather the storm.

KC: If you don't mind, can you please take us, the readers back to a time in your life when you got knocked down and you asked yourself why? How did that happen?

JD: There was a time in my life, in my day-to-day living I rarely had a place to stay.

KC: What do mean you didn't have a place to stay? When did that all begin?

JD: This started at the age of 18. My father lost his house and one night I slept on the floor of an abandon house during the winter months. For a while I would go from one place to another. I've been here and there ever since. I joined a gang when all of this stuff happen. I loved the feeling of brotherly love, respect, loyalty, and honor.

KC: When your father lost the house did it hurt you?

JD: Yes, I hurt me really bad. I actually cried.

KC: **So where did your father go after he lost the house?**

JD: He went to shelters. At one time we were going to the same shelters together. Interestingly, finally there came a moment when my father wanted to be a parent and show some form of love for me and became remorseful about the situation. That remorse lead him to feeling less than a man and father. He told me since he doesn't have a place to stay that maybe I'll do better without him and try to find a place on my own.

KC: **Did you ever give up?**

JD: Actually, I never give up! As bad and hurtful the situation was, I never gave up. Yes, I felt stuck in a dark place, hopeless, with no air. But I just kept pushing and I never gave up.

KC: **What techniques do you use to keep you from living life in park or reverse?**

JD: I go to church every week. I have friends by my side that understands my day-to-day living. I write things down in my journal. Life is getting better now. I'm very hopeful, because I am self-motivated.

KC: **What advice would you like to share with your fellow teen warriors?**

JD: I'm learning that in order to go forward in life, you have to plan to go forward. Lastly, I remember reading somewhere in the Bible that if you would always do the right things you will always proposer. Always do the right thing because you will proposer.

Reflective Exercise

"If you believe in yourself
anything is possible."
~Unknown

Over the next thirty (30) days the goal is to say each positive affirmation below three (3) times a day.

1.   I am a believer in myself.

2.   I am destined for greatness.

3.   I am bigger than my circumstances.

WALKING OPTIMISM

Sunny Rodriquez

KC: **Hey Sunny, thanks for joining me today.**

SR: What's up Mr. Cooper! Not a problem.

KC: **Ok Sunny, let's get right to it. Please share with us, the readers what stage in life you are currently living in.**

SR: I have been through a lot in life. For the most part, I am no longer trying to figure things out. I now know what I need to do to move on in life. I have plans and I'm not just thinking about the plans, I am putting them to action. There is no doubt that I am moving forward. Even when obstacles surround me. So, in your terms, I am in "Drive".

This is how I know I'm living in "drive". When I was younger, my father wasn't around. It was just my two brothers, my mom and I. My brothers and I all have different fathers. One brother left to go live with his father and my other brother kept getting kicked out of the house. My mother had her own issues suffering from mental illness; many times taking her issues out on us. So as a little kid not having my brothers, a father, or a positive male figure around, I pretty much was in the streets a lot.

At a very young age I started robbing people: it was easy. I was a little kid, no one expected it to be me. I would be out to 2 o'clock in the morning at such a young age. Eventually, someone called the cops on me and I was put into foster care. I went from foster care to foster care. I ran away a lot. I wasn't ever at one place for more than a year. I had friends, but never long term friends. I didn't trust people. I just couldn't understand why they took me away from my mother.

When I was 10 years old the courts awarded full custody of me to my father. The problem was, he was very abusive. He was a neglecter and physically abusive. He would choke me, submerge my head underwater in the bathtub, beat me with a 2x4; he was really abusive. But the neglect, I don't care what anyone says, to me neglect is the worst form of abuse that can happen to you. He would nail my windows shut. There were many times that he would leave me in my room with nothing on but my boxers. I was 10 for crying out loud! I would get in trouble for little things like going to bed and leaving the TV on. (Little stuff)

This is when my life really started to take a nose dive. So at 14 years old he kicked me out of the house. I was homeless for an entire year and I didn't want to tell anybody. I was so afraid to go back to foster care. Therefore, I was on my own and sleep on the streets. I started selling drugs. I don't drink. I don't smoke. I sold because I had to eat. At 14 I already understood that for certain things to go on in life you can't cry, you can't sit, or you can't wait or wish; you have to act. The longer you wait, the worst things were going to get. So I did what I had to do. I couldn't get a regular job at 14.

Even though I was doing what I thought I had to do to survive. I got caught. As a juvenile I been to jail about 15 times. I was in and out of jail. The interesting thing about jail, in a crazy way, it was what I wanted. I finally felt connected to people that were just like me. I know that sounds crazy, but it was true. There was this one time when

I was 15 that I got locked up for (5) counts of trafficking and (5) counts of possession. This time I spent 1 year in jail. After I got out that time, I said to myself I am not getting locked up again. I am not going to sell drugs again. I refuse to let other people control what I do or affect the way I think. That single statement was the beginning of me moving forward in life.

I like I said, I'm moving forward because I've grown. I would never be the person that I am today if didn't go into foster care. Going to foster care opened my mind. It made me start writing and reading at the level that I am writing and reading today.

KC: **Wow! It looks like foster care was a blessing in disguise.**

SR: It truly was.

KC: **Sunny, life is filled with metaphoric expressions. Some people use metaphors like a rollercoaster, garden, deck of cards, etc. to describe life. Does anyone of those apply to you or do you have your own?**

SR: My life is like the movie Grease and Antwone Fisher. Here's why, I've had some glorious moments that many of my peers haven't experienced and I've also had some unfortunately circumstances that my peers haven't experienced.

KC: **You've shared some of your life so far. But has there been an event that knocked you down emotionally?**

SR: It was the time my mother came to court for the final custody decision. This was the first time I seen her in years. So the final ruling was made by the judge awarding 100 percent custody to my father. After the ruling was made, during the case the judge asked my mom would you like to have any communication with your son? My mom says no! Do you want to call your son? No! Do you want the address of where your son will be residing so you can write your son? No! After the court case I went to go give my mother a hug and kiss she just stood there looking at me with disgust and walked away. That was the last time I seen my mother until 7 years later.

KC: **I'm sure you have heard people say, "I just had a eureka moment" or say "Ah Ha!" That being said, what triggered your move forward? What was your motivating factor?**

SR: Real simple, maturity. Maturity, especially as a man, being able to work through hard times. If you're still complaining you can't move forward in life.

KC: **What techniques do you use to keep yourself moving forward in life?**

SR: Knowing that there is something that would get me the same reward without the same consequences. 1) I could go rob someone for their Samsung Galaxy and get $500.00 and go to jail. Or option 2) depending on the season go knock on doors and shovel snow.

KC: **Sunny even while you tell your story, you still seem to be a happy person. I know you had some dark days but what about days that brought you some joy. We would love to learn about a life major accomplishment.**

SR: Honestly, life is one big major accomplishment. In addition to life being one major accomplishment, I have a 3.0 gpa (grade point average) after all that I been through. I joined two non-profits and have a job that I enjoy doing.

KC: **I've learned so much from you and your fellow teen warriors. But what advice**

would offer to your fellow teen warrior that feels like throwing in the towel, giving up and walking away?

SR: It's real simple. Be mature. You don't have to be more positive. Be mature and positive things will come.

Reflective Exercise

"The best is yet to come."
~Unknown

It's deposit time! It's time to make a deposit into your bank of optimism. The goal here is for you to make a daily deposit into your bank of optimism using one positive action per day. Below are seven deposit logs.

Monday: Have A Positive Attitude

Tuesday: Create Your Own Happiness

Wednesday: Maintain Your Confidence

Thursday: Remain Hopeful

Friday: Have Self-Trust

Saturday: Stay Cheerful

Sunday: Become Enthusiastic

PURPOSE BEHIND THE PASSION

Cindy Williams

KC: **Greetings Cindy, thank you so much for joining me today. It is an honor to sit down with the heart behind the organization Loving Arms, Inc. So, let get started. Cindy, what stage in life are you living in?**

CW: Drive, I do understand what my purpose is in life and I'm excited about that. For the first time in my life I know what it is that I am supposed to do and I'm excited about doing it. Every moment of my being is about doing this work. I can't think of anything else that I would like to do. This work of working with teens and families, bringing families to wholeness I believe, that's my calling and purpose in life.

KC: You said wholeness. What is your definition of wholeness?

CW: When I think about wholeness, I first think of its opposite, brokenness. I think that many people are broken now-a-days; especially the family. I love the work we are doing here at Loving Arms. At Loving Arms it's all about bringing families together. Rebuilding families who've been broken and torn apart by life challenges and situations. As well as hurt, abused, and neglected. We do this by helping those families really identify where they are and what their needs are. Once we do that, we then come together collectively to rebuild and bring families back together that have been broken apart.

KC: Where did the name Loving Arms come from?

CW: Back in 1999 when the organization was just a thought, I played with names and I thought about what was really crucial for me as a young person growing up. Honestly, it was the love that I felt from my parents. We were huggers. I still am today. Being embraced, there was safety in that. There is something about the love I felt when I was in my parent's arms that gave me the desire and drive to do. Everything I did I always felt like I can do anything and honestly they made me feel that way. They gave me the confidence to go and do things and not be afraid to fail. Even if did, I knew that they would be there to lift me up, support me, and protect me. So "Loving Arms" seem to be so appropriate. I didn't realize at the time that it also signify for me today all about what God represent for us. That in His arms we also find safe.

KC: **Cindy, you and your work specializes in giving from the essence of your heart. I'm sure it hasn't been easy. But is there anything about your life that you would change?**

CW: Life has been an experience. There is very little that I would change about life, because everything in my life has given me the experience needed to build on the next stage in my life. Everything that God has allowed to happen was to prepare me for the purpose in which I serve.

KC: **Although your work is very rewarding in the sense of rebuilding families. That in itself can be quite burdensome. So, what techniques do you use to keep moving forward?**

CW: Prayer, it's a lot. This work is not easy. (Pardon my tears) God is truly the source of my strength. Honestly, if it wasn't for God there's no way I could do this work.

By the way, my mom has been my greatest inspiration. She always encourages me to go and do; not only do, but do things to help other people.

KC: **Looking around at the great work that Loving Arms is doing, I know there's a list mile long of great accomplishments. But if you don't mind we would love if you could share a major accomplishment.**

CW: The fact that "Loving Arms" is making a difference; as much as I do get overwhelmed by what's going on, we are really doing this. That within itself is a major accomplishment.

KC: **With all the experience and knowledge that you have accumulated throughout your journey, what advice would you like to share to assist the teen warriors?**

CW: Okay, I have advice for teens and parents/ caregivers

For teens, always remember that all things are possible through Christ. That has been a life lesson for me as well. Also remember, to never give up and never quit! There were so many days that I was on the verge of giving up. There were so many times that I wanted to quit. Looking back I say to myself if I would have quit, none of this would have ever happened.

For parents or caregivers here is my advice. During our organization's open house someone asked me what do I think is needed to save our families today? I replied Love. The key to life is love.

Conclusion

Built To Last

Many would agree that one of the worst winters that this country has had in decades and possibly centuries occurred during the 2013-2014 winter season. There were record lows throughout the nation. Not only were temperatures below freezing throughout many parts of the country, it seems as if every week there was a major snow storm. As soon as we got through one, here came another. Mentally, it really took a toll on us as a nation.

During one of those below freezing days, while taking my children to school. My youngest daughter Kahzire said with deep concern in her voice, "I feel sorry for the trees. They are freezing." She then asked, "Who's going to take care of them?" She was very concerned. Khia my oldest daughter said, "yeah, you're right, I'm sure they are cold. But don't worry, because they were built to last." Right then and there, her simple, yet powerful statement stopped me in my mental tracks. After thinking about it for a brief moment, I came to the same conclusion as Khia. She's right! The same tree that I saw in the summer is the same tree that I saw in the fall. The same tree that I saw in the fall is the same tree that I saw in the winter. And the same tree that I saw in the winter was the same exact tree that I saw in the spring. That same tree made it through season, after season, after season. Here is the good news. You and I are similar to the tree. We were built to last. You were built to last. You were created to endure and enjoy the different seasons and stages in life.

Here is a clear indication that you were built to last. Think about the different things that you may have experienced in your life so far. You may have lost a parent, a family member, or a close friend. You may have battled a certain health related issue. You may have been abused verbally, physically, mentally, sexually or emotionally. You may have experienced homelessness or being bullied. Whatever the situation may have been, guess what, you are still here. See, I told you that you were built to last.

During certain seasons the tree begins to change. Let's look at the fall season first. The leaves changes many different vibrant colors and eventually begin to fall from the tree. By the time winter arrives the tree may be completely bare. For many of us when we go through the winter season of our life it doesn't feel good. It feels as if the season is never going to end. It's one thing after another. Sometimes you just want to give up but when you feel like that, think about the trees.

Although the tree may have lost its leaves and the birds and squirrels have abandoned it, the tree does not hold its branches down in shame. It doesn't up root itself because of depression and anger. The tree stands there with its branches straight out knowing that regardless what season it is, it is still a tree and it was built to last. The same goes for you, teen warrior. No matter who stays or leaves, in the end you were built to last. Stretch your mind, believe in yourself. Become the person that you were created to be. You are great. You are special. You are a winner. You are a warrior. Keep in mind that no matter what, declare out loud, "I was built to last!"

Your Life's Reflection

1. What stage am I in now?

    _____

2. What stage would I like to be in six (6) months?

    _____

3. What stage would like to be in one (1) year?

    _____

Here are three (3) simple tips to help you achieve your ultimate goal of "living life in drive."

DECIDE: Of the three tips, this is the most important tip. Ben Stein asserted, *"The first step to getting the things you want out of life is this: decide what you want and go be it."* Today, make up your mind and choose your life's direction. Take a few moments of alone time and choose exactly what you want out of life. Always remember that nothing can or has ever been accomplished without first making a decision.

VISUALIZE: This is the second most important tip. This is your time to use your imagination and create your own mental movie. Close your eyes and see yourself achieving your goals in life. This process does not require a lot of time; a few minutes a day will do the trick. For best results, try to find a quiet place or a quiet time while you are visualizing. Keep in mind, "if you can imagine it and visualize it, you can create it."

CONQUER: This is the last tip that will help you on your journey to "live life in drive." Now that you have decided your life's direction and visualized yourself getting there. The next step is to take action and make it happen. Ultimately, there are three kinds of people in the world that we live in.

1. **People that let life happen.** This group has not yet decided to "live life in drive." Instead they have allowed life to control them. They just let life happen.

2. **People that ask what happen.** Instead of being in the game of life, this group of people decides to stand on the sidelines of life not having a clue of what's going on in their life. Matter of fact,

they have decided to settle right where they are; becoming complacent and lazy.

3. **People that make things happen.** This group are the Steve Jobs. The LeBron James. The Sean "Diddy" Combs. The J.K Rowling's. The Reese Witherspoon's. The Oprah's of the world. As well as, the teens in this book. And especially you! This group refuses to settle for second best. This group of individuals strive to always make things happen. They never make excuses. They only make progress. You are no different than them. And they are no different than you. They **decided**. They **visualized**. They **conquered**! And so will you!

National Resource List

Below is a national resource list for possible usage to assist you on your journey of "living life in drive"!

Loving Arm's Inc.
www.lovingarmsinc.com
443-415-1174

American Foundation for Suicide Prevention
www.afsp.org
1800-273-8255

Safe Place
www.nationalsafeplace.org
1800-786-2929

The National Domestic Violence Hotline
www.thehotline.org
1800-799-7233

American Pregnancy Hotline
www.thehelpline.org
1866-942-6466

National Eating Disorders Association

www.nationaleatingdisorders.org

1800-931-2237

Partnership for Drug-Free Kids

www.drugfree.org

1-855-378-4373

Thursday's Child

www.thursdayschild.org

1800-872-5437

The Trevor Project

www.thetrevorproject.org

1866-488-7386

Child Help

www.childhelp.org

1800-422-4453

About The Author

Kashaun Cooper Sr. was born in New York City – the eldest of three siblings. At the age of six, he experienced an event that would change his life forever. This event caused him to spend his tender years growing up without the presence of his father. However, it was Kashaun's tenacity and passion to make a difference that led him to start the non-profit organization – Fathers Rock, Inc.

As Founder & Chairman of The Champion Father and Father's Rock, Inc., Kashaun has established and developed these organizations to empower fathers, children, teens, families and communities around the world.

Kashaun Cooper is an exceptional author and motivational speaker who has the ability to bring out the best in every individual. He has written two other books (*"What If I Am? The Four Stages In Life"* & *"The Champion Father"*) that have created a transformation in the lives of individuals around the world. His work has appeared in numerous national publications. Mr. Cooper speaks at Universities, schools, profit and non-profit organizations, radio shows and seminars around the country. He has served as vice president of the non-profit organization "Teen Dads Fresh Start." Kashaun has led and initiated many male involvement programs and launched a very successful annual back to school teen summit, sponsored by Radio One, 92Q Radio Station and Mondawmin Mall.

In addition, he co-founded and co-host the number one radio program in the region "Power to Push" and is a premier motivational speaker bringing motivational moments to catapult people into taking action. Recently, Mr. Cooper was nominated by "The Baltimore Times" for his extraordinary contributions and unique place in the civic life of Baltimore where he will be recognized as one of "50 Baltimore Men on the Move". He is also featured as a community hero by RadioOne/NewsOne/InteractiveOne. Most importantly, Kashaun is a committed Champion Father to his children.

Made in the USA
Charleston, SC
10 August 2014